10 GOALS

10 WELL-BEING GOALS

JANE BURNARD • FATTI BURKE

PowerKiDS press

Published in 2027
by The Rosen Publishing Group, Inc.
2544 Clinton Street, Buffalo, NY 14224

First published in Great Britain in 2023 by Wayland

Credits

Editor: Julia Bird

Editorial, design and project management: Raspberry Books

Design: Intrepid Books LTD

Illustrations: Fatti Burke

Note to parents and teachers: every effort has been made by the Publishers to ensure websites are suitable for children, that they are of the highest educational value, and that they contain no inappropriate or offensive material. However, because of the nature of the Internet, it is impossible to guarantee that the contents of these sites will not be altered. We strongly advise that Internet access is supervised by a responsible adult.

Please note that some of the foods mentioned in this book are allergens or may contain allergens. Please check any ingredients carefully if you have a known food allergy to avoid an allergic reaction.

This book also contains tips on exercise and other activities. With any new activity, start off gently and build up slowly to avoid injury.

The website addresses (URLs) included in this book were valid at the time of going to press. However, it is possible that contents or addresses may have changed since the publication of this book. No responsibility for any such changes can be accepted by either the author or the Publisher.

Cataloging-in-Publication Data

Names: Burnard, Jane, author. | Burke, Fatti, illustrator.
Title: 10 well-being goals / written by Jane Burnard, illustrated by Fatti Burke.
Description: Buffalo, New York : PowerKids Press, 2027. | Series: 10 goals | Includes glossary and index.
Identifiers: ISBN 9781499459180 (pbk.) | ISBN 9781499459197 (library bound) | ISBN 9781499459203 (ebook)
Subjects: LCSH: Self-care, Health--Juvenile literature. | Well-being--Juvenile literature. |
Mind and body--Juvenile literature.
Classification: LCC RA777.B876 2027 | DDC 613--dc23

Printed in China

CPSIA Compliance Information: Batch #QS27PK. For further information contact Rosen Publishing at 1-800-237-9932.

CONTENTS

Go for it, and good luck with achieving your 10 WELL-BEING GOALS!

WHY WELL-BEING GOALS ARE GOOD

Do you want to achieve 10 goals to make yourself happier and healthier? Then read on.

Well-being means living our best lives – feeling healthy and happy, having enough good food to eat, somewhere safe to live, going to school, being looked after, and having friends. It also means being able to achieve our goals – whether that's learning to skateboard, getting better at football, or feeling confident and at ease with ourselves.

We're all special, unique people, with different needs and abilities. But by looking after our own well-being, we can live happily in the present and look forward confidently towards the future.

This book contains loads of helpful information, advice and activities to meet 10 Well-Being Goals – from eating and sleeping well to dealing with stress, enjoying time with friends or by yourself and being kind to others. Achieving your well-being goals is the perfect way to set yourself on the right track for health and happiness.

GOAL 1

EAT WELL

We need to eat well to be well. Eating good food nourishes your mind as well as your body.

So here's a handy guide to healthy food – and some things you might want to avoid.

EAT AS MUCH FRUIT AND VEGGIES AS YOU CAN. THEY CONTAIN NATURAL VITAMINS AND MINERALS THAT PROTECT OUR BODIES FROM DISEASE AND KEEP US HEALTHY.

Eat plenty of carbohydrates, such as whole grain bread, potatoes in their skins, brown rice, and pasta for energy.

EAT SOME PROTEIN, LIKE BEANS, FISH, EGGS, AND MEAT, EVERY DAY. PROTEIN BUILDS AND PROTECTS BONES AND MUSCLES, AND HELPS US GROW.

HAVE SOME OF THESE TOO:

Good fats, like those in nuts, seeds, and olive oil, help us absorb vitamins, protect our bones and organs, and keep our hearts healthy.

DAIRY PRODUCTS LIKE MILK AND CHEESE, AND NON-DAIRY ALTERNATIVES SUCH AS OAT MILK, GIVE US MINERALS LIKE CALCIUM THAT BUILD BONES.

LIMIT HOW MUCH OF THESE YOU EAT!

Stuff with added sugar, including sugary drinks and breakfast cereals, candy, cakes, cookies, and chocolate.

JUNK FOOD, SUCH AS BURGERS AND FRIES, CONTAINS A LOT OF SUGAR, SALT, AND THE WRONG KINDS OF FAT. IT DOESN'T GIVE US THE NUTRIENTS WE NEED AND IT DOESN'T ALWAYS FILL US UP.

TOP TIPS FOR EATING WELL

Here are some great ways to make sure we get all the nutrients we need.

1 DON'T SKIP BREAKFAST

STUDIES SHOW THAT CHILDREN WHO EAT BREAKFAST DO BETTER IN SCHOOL TESTS THAN THOSE WHO DON'T! TRY FRESH OR DRIED FRUIT, TOAST, AND NON-SUGARY CEREALS WITH MILK OR NON-DAIRY MILK ALTERNATIVES.

2 JAZZ UP YOUR VEGGIES

Fruit and vegetables are nature's superfoods, so eat lots. If you find raw veggies boring, try dipping them in delicious hummus, tahini, or tzatziki.

3 SNACK HEALTHILY

SNACKS LIKE CHIPS, CANDY, AND CHOCOLATE CONTAIN LOTS OF UNHEALTHY FAT, SALT, AND SUGAR. BUT SNACKING ON FRUIT AND VEGGIES HELPS TO KEEP US HEALTHY AND HAPPY!

4 DRINK ENOUGH

Did you know the human body is 75 percent water? We need to keep topped up by drinking 6 to 8 cups of water, fruit juice, milk, or tea a day.

5 EAT A RAINBOW!

A WIDE RANGE OF HEALTHY FOODS, WITH DIFFERENT COLORS, TEXTURES, AND TASTES, MEANS WE GET A WIDE RANGE OF NUTRIENTS TOO!

It's not just what we eat that makes us healthy, but how. Try to sit down and eat with family or friends at the same times each day – don't rush your food, and turn off the TV!

GOAL 2

SLEEP WELL

Why do we sleep? It's a bit of a mystery. No one knows the whole reason! But here's what we DO know:

Melatonin (the "sleep hormone") makes us feel sleepy. It triggers our body clocks in the evening, letting us know it's time for bed.

SLEEP IMPROVES OUR MEMORIES. WHILE OUR BODIES REST, OUR BRAIN IS BUSY SORTING OUT THE DAY'S EVENTS AND FEELINGS AND STORING THEM.

Sleep helps our bodies repair themselves.

A GOOD NIGHT'S SLEEP MAKES US FEEL ENERGIZED AND ALERT THE NEXT DAY.

Sleep improves our concentration, attention, and ability to learn.

SLEEP KEEPS OUR HEARTS HEALTHY AND STRENGTHENS OUR IMMUNE SYSTEMS.

So, sleep's a pretty good thing! How can we make sure we get enough of it? Turn the page for some top tips.

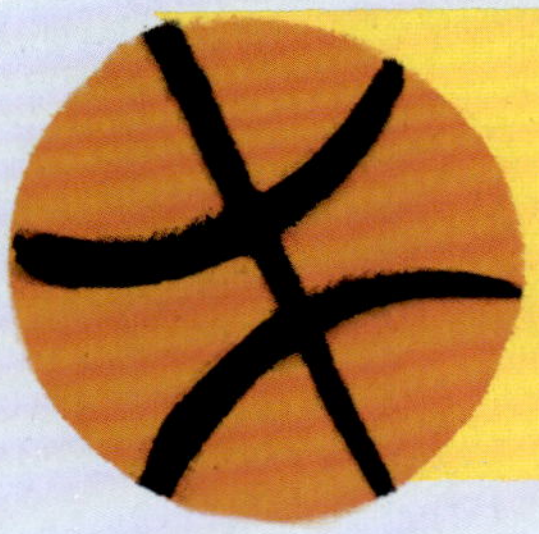

TOP TIPS FOR

Young people need about ten hours of sleep a night. Here's how to get just that.

1 BE ACTIVE DURING THE DAY

AN ACTIVE DAY MAKES US NATURALLY TIRED SO WE SLEEP WELL AT NIGHT.

2 GET INTO A ROUTINE

Doing the same things in the same order at the same time every morning and night helps us fall asleep more quickly.

3 SET THE SCENE

THICK CURTAINS OR BLINDS HELP KEEP THE LIGHT OUT. DIM LIGHTING MAKES US FEEL SLEEPY, AND A TIDY ROOM MAKES US FEEL RELAXED! MAKE SURE YOUR ROOM'S NOT TOO HOT, OR TOO COLD. ABOUT 65° F (18° C) IS GOOD.

SLEEPING WELL

4 AVOID SCREENS

Tablets, smartphones, TVs, and other electronic gadgets produce "blue light" from their screens, which can fool the body into thinking it's daytime. So switch off your devices at night and charge your phone in another room. Make your bedroom a screen-free zone!

5 EAT AND DRINK WELL

Sugar, caffeine (found in tea, coffee, sodas, and energy drinks) and chocolate are stimulants, which keep us awake. So make sure you avoid these at least six hours before bedtime.

6 READ QUIETLY OR LISTEN TO RELAXING MUSIC IN BED

TRY SOUNDS LIKE BIRDSONG, WAVES, THE PATTER OF RAIN, OR WATERFALLS AND RIVERS TO SOOTHE YOU TO SLEEP.

GOAL 3

RELAX

Make relaxation part of your day and enjoy wonderful results.

Take a deep breath in ... now let it out, nice and slowly ... let your muscles go all floppy and feel the smile spread across your face.

It's time to calm right down, let your busy brain switch off for a while, and relax.

So many good things happen when we relax. Here are just a few.

We breathe more deeply, taking in more oxygen. This oxygen flows around our body, dissolving the tension in our muscles and relieving pain.

Our heart rate and breathing slow down, making us feel calm.

OUR BLOOD CIRCULATION AND IMMUNE SYSTEMS GET STRONGER, HELPING US FIGHT CONDITIONS SUCH AS THE COMMON COLD.

OUR MINDS ARE CALMER AND CLEARER. THIS HELPS US THINK POSITIVELY AND CONCENTRATE, PLUS IT IMPROVES OUR MEMORY AND PROBLEM-SOLVING SKILLS.

We feel less stressed and it helps keep our emotions in check – making us feel less angry and sad.

Even better, relaxing is something we can all do – and it's really easy. Learning to be mindful, being in nature, reading, listening to soothing music, doing hobbies that let us express ourselves, or just having a quiet time on our own – these are all ways to relax.

TOP TIPS TO RELAX

So how do we relax? Here are some ideas.

1 WATCH YOUR BREATHING

Sit down in a comfortable, quiet place. Close your eyes and your mouth, concentrate on the tip of your nose, and feel the breath coming in and out, naturally. When your mind wanders, don't worry, just bring it back again. This helps you to be mindful – which means being in the moment.

2 BLOW SOME BUBBLES!

WHEN WE BLOW SOAP BUBBLES, WE CAN'T BLOW TOO HARD (THE BUBBLES WILL POP) OR TOO SOFTLY (WE WON'T MAKE ANY!). BY BLOWING SOMEWHERE IN THE MIDDLE AND MAKING PERFECT BUBBLES, WE LEARN HOW TO BREATHE CALMLY AND RELAX.

3 STRETCH IT OUT

RELEASE THE TENSION IN YOUR MUSCLES BY STRE-E-E-ETCHING THEM OUT! TRY THIS. SLOWLY STRETCH YOUR ARMS ABOVE YOUR HEAD, STANDING AS TALL AS POSSIBLE, THEN LET THEM FLOP BACK DOWN.

4 CLOUD SPOT

Lie on your back outside and watch the clouds as they float above.

5 DOODLE, DRAW OR COLOR IN

LET YOUR CREATIVITY FLOW! CRAFTS AND HOBBIES LIKE KNITTING, SEWING, AND JIGSAW PUZZLES ARE GOOD FOR CREATIVITY AND MINDFULNESS TOO.

6 DO WHAT YOU LOVE

Do things you enjoy, like listening to relaxing music, or reading your favorite books.

Learning how to relax is a skill that helps us throughout our lives, especially if we feel stressed.

GOAL 4

ORGANIZE YOUR BEDROOM

What do you see in your bedroom?

a) Everything neatly in its place.
or
b) a mish-mash of clutter everywhere?

If the answer's b), this is the goal for you. And even if it's a), you'll find some handy tips to be even more organized!

Organizing doesn't mean shoving everything into closets then breathing a sigh of relief. It means sorting through things and making decisions about where they should go. Do you really want that crumpled-up painting you did four years ago? Or the odd sock that doesn't fit any more? And where should you put the things you do want to keep?

THE IDEA OF ORGANIZING YOUR ROOM MIGHT MAKE YOUR HEART SINK, BUT IT'S GUARANTEED TO MAKE YOU FEEL GOOD.

When we declutter, organize, and clean up we:

USE OUR DECISION-MAKING AND PROBLEM-SOLVING SKILLS.

GIVE OURSELVES SOME HEAD-SPACE – BEING IN AN UNTIDY PLACE CAN MAKE US FEEL STRESSED AND LESS ABLE TO CONCENTRATE.

Help our family, friends, and community by sharing possessions we don't need any more.

Feel a sense of self-esteem and make more dopamine – a happiness hormone!

Now let's get **ORGANIZING!**

TOP TIPS FOR ORGANIZING YOUR BEDROOM

Follow these tips for a tidy new bedroom.

1 TELL YOUR PARENT OR CARER WHAT YOU'RE DOING

THEY MIGHT WANT A SAY IN WHAT YOU GIVE AWAY OR THROW OUT!

2 MAKE IT FUN!

Put on some music and/or have a friend come by to help.

3 DECLUTTER

Label three boxes "Put Away," "Give Away," and "Recycle." Start with one part of your room. This could be your desk, your dresser, or closet. Take everything out, look at each object and ask yourself a) whether you use it regularly, and b) whether it makes you happy. If the answer is yes to either, it goes in the Put Away box. The Give Away box is for things in good condition that can go to family, friends, or charity. The Recycle box is for anything that's broken, torn, or beyond repair. Most things can be recycled at local donation centers, but check first.

4 ORGANIZE

NOW PUT EVERYTHING IN ORDER! HERE ARE SOME IDEAS.

- KEEP LOOSE PAPERS IN FILES AND BOXES.
- SEE-THROUGH PLASTIC BOXES ARE GREAT FOR STORAGE, BECAUSE YOU CAN SEE WHAT'S IN THEM.
- PUT DRAWER DIVIDERS IN YOUR DRAWERS, TO STOP ALL THOSE PENS, PENCILS, AND OTHER THINGS FROM GETTING MUDDLED UP.

Check out your new-look, **organized** bedroom, and feel **proud**!

GOAL 5

BE ACTIVE

Did you know that being active is a foolproof way to feel good – both physically and mentally? And it's so easy! All you need is sixty minutes a day. Those sixty minutes can be split up throughout the day if you like – ten minutes here, ten minutes there.

You can be active in any way you like – as long as it makes your heart beat faster.

Here's what happens when we get active:

We build strong muscles and bones – which is really important when we're still growing.

WE MAINTAIN A HEALTHY WEIGHT.

OUR IMMUNE SYSTEMS GET STRONGER, SO WE'RE LESS LIKELY TO GET ILL.

We sleep better.

Studies show that we feel happier, more confident, and less stressed.

GOING FOR A TEN-MINUTE JOG CAN PUT YOU IN A GOOD MOOD WHICH LASTS FOR SEVERAL HOURS!

Practicing a skill, like skateboarding or playing basketball, makes us feel great as we get better at it.

And don't worry – not everyone loves playing team sports. Some don't even like *any* sports! That's fine. There's still loads you can do. Turn over for some top tips.

TOP TIPS FOR BEING ACTIVE

Let's get those hearts pumping!

1 WALK OR CYCLE TO AND FROM SCHOOL

You can also use a skateboard, scooter, rollerblades, or wheelchair! You'll be doing the environment a favor by not using fossil-fuel-powered vehicles. Litter-picking as you go, with a parent or carer, is another great way to be active and help the environment too.

2 SWIM

Swimming develops strength, balance, and confidence, plus it keeps us healthy and fit. Sign up for lessons if you can, and remember to only swim in safe, supervised places.

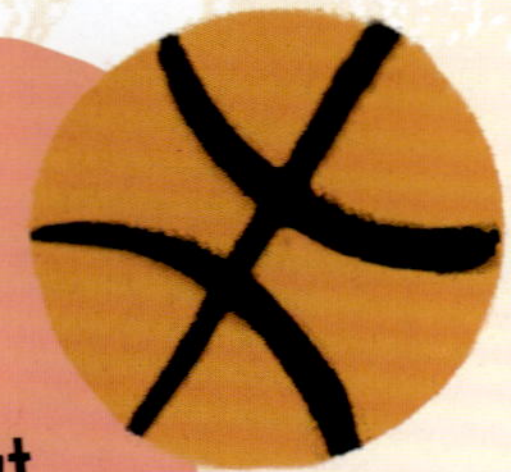

3 TRY SOMETHING NEW

Discover new hobbies and skills! How about karate, judo, or table tennis? Joining a school sports team can also be good way to get active and have fun.

4 BE ACTIVE INDOORS

- TIDYING YOUR BEDROOM, HELPING TO CLEAN THE KITCHEN, OR HANGING OUT THE LAUNDRY CAN ALL BE ACTIVE EXERCISE.

- TURN YOURSELF AND YOUR FAMILY FROM COUCH POTATOES TO JUMPING BEANS BY MAKING TV COMMERCIAL BREAKS INTO STAR-JUMP CONTESTS!

- HAVE A KITCHEN DISCO! TURN UP THE MUSIC AND GET DANCING – THE WILDER THE BETTER!

5 MAKE IT FUN

Skipping is a great full-body workout that improves stamina and coordination. Juggling and/or hula-hooping can keep you fit AND impress your friends! And running or walking with family or friends is a great way to enjoy your green spaces.

If all this is new to you, don't worry. Start slow, go at your own pace, keep at it and have fun!

GOAL 6

ENJOY FRIENDSHIPS

Friends are great company. We can't wait to see them and we love doing things with them. We can tell them all our secrets, and be sure they'll keep them.

Friends celebrate our successes and special times, and they cheer us up when we're down. Hooray for friends!

GOOD FRIENDS:

KEEP US COMPANY AND STOP US FEELING LONELY.

Listen to us. When we feel stressed, talking to a caring friend makes us feel better *and* helps us find ways to solve our problems.

Support us when times are tough – such as when moving to a new house, or when we're having family problems.

WITH A GREAT FRIEND BEHIND YOU, YOU CAN TAKE ON THE WORLD! WHEN FRIENDS CHEER US ON, WE FEEL SELF-CONFIDENT AND ABLE TO ACHIEVE OUR GOALS.

Even better, friendship is a two-way street. When we are kind to our friends, it makes us feel good too. Plus, with friends we develop the gift of empathy, which means understanding and sharing another person's feelings.

HAVING STRONG FRIENDSHIPS HAS ACTUALLY BEEN PROVED TO MAKE YOU LIVE LONGER!

So let's make the most of friends!

TOP TIPS FOR BEING A GOOD FRIEND

These tips will guide you towards happy, successful friendships.

1 SPEND QUALITY TIME TOGETHER

Try joining an after-school club, a sports team, an art or crafting class, or a nature group with your friends. This is also a great way to make NEW friends!

2 STOP, LOOK, AND LISTEN

PEOPLE WARM TO FRIENDS WHO LISTEN WELL. WHEN SOMEONE SPEAKS TO YOU: **STOP** WHAT YOU'RE DOING AND GIVE THEM YOUR FULL ATTENTION, **LOOK** AT THEM AND SMILE, **LISTEN** CAREFULLY TO WHAT THEY SAY AND **WAIT** UNTIL THEY FINISH BEFORE YOU REPLY.

3 SHOW YOU'RE INTERESTED

Find out more about your friends by asking questions, like "What has been your happiest moment?" "If you could be an animal, what would you be, and why?" Or "Would you rather go to space or to the bottom of the sea?"

4 GIVE COMPLIMENTS

ARE YOUR FRIENDS ... CLEVER? CARING? FUNNY? BRAVE? LOYAL? FULL OF BRILLIANT IDEAS? BE SURE TO TELL THEM!

Be there for your friends in good times and bad. Do all you can to support and help them if they're feeling down.

It doesn't really matter how many friends you have. One or two really good friends are better than loads of acquaintances you hardly know.

GOAL 7

LOVE NATURE

Where's your nearest green space? Is it a garden, park, or nature reserve? Wherever it is, get out there – because being outside, surrounded by trees, plants, wild animals, and birds makes us feel GOOD!

The colors of a park full of summer flowers, the smell of freshly-cut grass, the sound of birds singing, and the feel of autumn leaves under our feet – all these fill us with wonder and a desire to explore and learn more.

GREEN SPACES MAKE US:

SMARTER – JUST 20 MINUTES SPENT IN NATURE IMPROVES CONCENTRATION.

STRONGER – BELIEVE IT OR NOT, RESEARCH HAS PROVED THAT RUNNING AROUND, JUMPING, AND CLIMBING OUTDOORS IN GREEN SPACES DOES MORE GOOD THAN THE SAME AMOUNT OF EXERCISE INDOORS!

HEALTHIER – a 30-minute visit to a park can make our hearts fitter, and walking in nature boosts our immune systems, making us less likely to get ill.

HAPPIER – just a five-minute walk in nature improves our mood, making us feel relaxed. And the more time we spend there, the happier we are!

Nature has such a positive effect on us that even just looking at photos of nature can lower our stress levels, as can being close to house plants!

TOP TIPS TO

Here are some good ideas for enjoying the great outdoors.

2 KEEP A NATURE DIARY

BECOME AN EXPERT NATURALIST AND MAKE A NOTE OF ALL THE FLOWERS, BIRDS, AND ANIMALS YOU'VE SEEN, TOGETHER WITH WHEN AND WHERE.

1 GO ON A NATURE TREK

Talk to an adult about going on a nature trek with a warden or park ranger in a local park or nature reserve. There'll be loads of other great activities too, like den-building, making camp fires, and climbing trees.

3 GO POND DIPPING

Ponds are magnets for insects and amphibians like frogs, toads, and newts. Ask an adult to go pond dipping with you in your nearest pond. Keep safe around water. Be very careful as the edge of a pond can be slippery. Don't lean out across water.

LOVE NATURE

4 GO ON A BUG HUNT

GENTLY LIFT AN OLD, ROTTEN PIECE OF WOOD AND LOOK UNDERNEATH. YOU'RE BOUND TO SEE SOME AMAZING CREEPY-CRAWLIES!

5 CREATE SOME NATURE ART

Get arty with leaves, sticks, and stones, draw or paint a wild place, or take some photos. Or how about writing a nature poem about your favorite wild animal?

6 MAKE A WILDLIFE ZONE

AT HOME OR AT SCHOOL, PLANT INSECT-FRIENDLY FLOWERS THAT BEES LOVE TO FEED ON, LEAVE UNMOWN AREAS FOR WILDLIFE, FEED BIRDS, AND MAKE BUG HOTELS (FIND OUT HOW ON THE INTERNET). YOU DON'T NEED A GARDEN – A BALCONY CAN BE A HAVEN FOR WILDLIFE.

But most of all, enjoy yourself!

GOAL 8

DEAL WELL WITH STRESS

Stress is what we feel when we're worried or uncomfortable about something. Like the sick feeling you might have before a school test, or the fear we get when we hear the people we love arguing.

Stress can make us feel sad, anxious, afraid, angry, and irritable.

Stress isn't always bad. A little bit of stress, now and then, can actually be helpful. Like the butterflies we feel when we have to do a class presentation or when we're in a room full of people we don't know. This kind of "good" stress can push us to do our best – to work hard for the presentation and to be friendly to new people.

HOWEVER, "BAD" STRESS IS GNAWING, ANXIOUS FEELINGS THAT GO ON FOR A LONG TIME – THIS KIND OF STRESS CAN END UP MAKING US ILL.

Luckily, there's a lot we can do to combat bad stress. In fact, every single one of the other goals in this book helps us deal better with it! So you're well on your way already.

THERE ARE LOTS OF OTHER WAYS TO COPE WITH STRESS TOO. TURN THE PAGE TO FIND OUT MORE.

TOP TIPS TO DEAL

When you feel stressed out, here are some practical things you can do to help yourself.

1 Talk to someone who's a good listener about the things that are bothering you and how they make you feel. This might be someone your own age or an adult you trust, like a parent or a teacher. Together, you can try to problem solve by understanding yourself and your reactions better. Sharing our problems with caring people always helps, even if the situation is too difficult to fix at once.

2 TAKE YOUR MIND OFF IT BY DOING SOMETHING YOU ENJOY OR ARE GOOD AT. THIS MIGHT BE RIDING YOUR BIKE, READING, OR A HOBBY LIKE PAINTING OR BIRD-WATCHING. HELPING SOMEONE ELSE WORKS TOO (SEE GOAL 9 FOR IDEAS ON BEING KIND TO OTHERS).

WELL WITH STRESS

3 Set aside time each day for relaxing. Look back at the Relax Goal for all the ways you can bring calmness and relaxation into your life. Then, just as you set aside time for school, homework, eating, and sleeping, make a space in your day for one of these. For instance, you could watch your breathing (see Goal 3) for a few minutes every night before you sleep.

Getting enough sleep, eating healthy food, exercising, having fun with good friends, and being in nature all help you handle stress too!

GOAL 9

BE KIND

When was the last time someone was kind to you? How did you feel? The answer is likely to be "Great!" But did you know that when we're kind to others, we feel just as great ourselves?

Scientists have proved that giving a gift can have the same effect on our brains as receiving one or eating our favorite food! This makes kindness a warm, wonderful, two-way thing.

More amazing facts about kindness:

When we give or receive kindness we make a "kindness hormone" called oxytocin. It makes us feel happy and content, and it brings our stress levels down.

KINDNESS IS CONTAGIOUS! WHEN YOU'RE KIND TO SOMEONE, THAT PERSON IS MORE LIKELY TO BE KIND TO ANOTHER PERSON. AND SO IS THAT PERSON, AND THE NEXT. BEFORE YOU KNOW IT, YOU'VE STARTED A KINDNESS EPIDEMIC!

Kindness makes us healthier. It boosts our immune systems and decreases our stress levels, making us less likely to get ill, plus it helps to keep our hearts healthy.

KINDNESS ACTS LIKE A BRAIN WORKOUT. WHEN WE'RE KIND, CERTAIN REGIONS OF THE BRAIN ARE EXERCISED. AND IF WE KEEP BEING KIND, THESE "KINDNESS MUSCLES" GROW BIGGER, MAKING US EVEN KINDER.

You're probably a kind person already. But how about being even kinder? Turn the page and find out how!

TOP TIPS FOR BEING KIND

Here are just a few ways to be kind.

1 MAKE IT A HABIT

Be kind to someone every day, whether it's clearing the table without being asked, playing with a younger sibling, helping your teacher, or being friendly to a new kid at school.

2 SHOW GRATITUDE

THINK ABOUT A TIME WHEN SOMEONE WAS KIND TO YOU. NEXT TIME YOU SEE THEM, THANK THEM FOR IT. SAY THANK YOU TO PEOPLE WHO DO THINGS FOR YOU BUT AREN'T ALWAYS THANKED, FOR EXAMPLE, YOUR TEACHER, OR SCHOOL CAFETERIA WORKER. BEING GRATEFUL DOES US JUST AS MUCH GOOD AS BEING KIND.

3 TRAIN YOUR BRAIN

Try this meditation once a day. It makes the kindness regions of the brain grow!

★ Find somewhere quiet and sit down comfortably.

★ Close your eyes, smile, and say the following three times (usually in your head): "May I be filled with loving kindness, peace, harmony, and happiness."

★ Then swap the "I" for someone you're close to, like your mom or your best friend.

★ Next, swap this name for a "neutral" person – like someone in your class that you don't know very well.

★ Now swap this one for a person you don't get on with that well.

★ Lastly, say "all beings," which includes all the people and animals on the Earth.

You can keep the same names each time, or choose different people. But always start with yourself and end with "all beings" and remember to say each line three times.

Kindness always COUNTS!

GOAL 10

FEEL HAPPY

What makes you happy? Can you think of the people, the places and the situations that put you in a happy mood?

You're probably smiling as you think of them – because smiling and laughter are signs of happiness, too.

Feeling happy does us so much good. When we're happy we're more able to think creatively and be open to information and ideas. It does those around us good too, because when we feel happy we're likely to be kind and friendly to others. Plus it makes us healthier – happy people live longer, have fewer aches and pains and feel less stress.

So how can we be even happier, and feel even better?

BY FOLLOWING THE GOALS IN THIS BOOK! PLUS . . .

LOOKING FOR WHAT'S GOOD. THIS MEANS THINKING POSITIVELY! WE CAN ACTUALLY TRAIN OUR BRAINS TO LOOK FOR THE GOOD THINGS, RATHER THAN THE BAD THINGS, IN EVERY SITUATION.

Celebrating our own good qualities. None of us are perfect, but knowing and making the most of our strengths makes us happy.

SMILING (EVEN IF YOU DON'T ALWAYS FEEL LIKE IT). THIS "TRICKS" YOUR MIND INTO FEELING HAPPINESS. SO DOES LAUGHING! AND BOTH SPREAD HAPPINESS TO OTHERS.

By keeping these aims in mind, we can look forward positively and with confidence.

TOP TIPS FOR

Remember, no one is happy *all* the time! Ups and downs are part of life. But by developing happiness skills, we give ourselves the tools to get through difficult times. Try these simple activities.

1 LEARN SOMETHING NEW!

MAYBE YOU'D LOVE TO PLAY GUITAR, TRY A NEW SPORT, OR LEARN HOW TO KNIT. GO FOR IT! WHEN WE LEARN A NEW SKILL, WE LOOK FORWARD IN A POSITIVE WAY.

Positive-thinking tip:
instead of saying "I can't do this" or "I'm not good at this" – add the word "yet." "I can't do this yet" or "I'm not good at this yet."

FEELING HAPPY

2 COUNT THE POSITIVES

Every night before you go to sleep, write down three things you enjoyed or were grateful for during the day. Even if it's as small as petting the cat! This helps your brain look for and focus on the positive things. People who did this activity for one week felt a happiness boost for up to six months.

3 LIST THE GOOD THINGS

WRITE DOWN WHAT YOU'RE GOOD AT AND REASONS TO FEEL PROUD OF YOURSELF. THINK OF AS MANY THINGS AS YOU CAN!

GREAT WORK!

By now you've probably realized that all the Well-Being Goals are linked. Being kind helps us feel happy, being happy helps us feel relaxed, being relaxed helps us deal with stress ... Every goal in this book is part of the circle of well-being – and now you're part of it too.

GLOSSARY

AMPHIBIAN – small animals, such as frogs, toads, and newts, that spend part of their life cycle in water.

BLUE LIGHT – the light produced by electronic screens.

CAFFEINE – a natural chemical found in tea, coffee, cola, and chocolate. It's a stimulant, which means too much of it can make you feel jumpy and nervous.

CARBOHYDRATES – an important source of energy in a healthy diet, found in starchy foods like potatoes, pasta and rice.

CONFIDENCE – the feeling of being sure of yourself and your abilities.

CREATIVITY – the ability to make new things or think of new ideas.

DAIRY PRODUCTS – any food made from animal milk.

DECLUTTER – remove or cut down on mess or clutter.

DOPAMINE – a neurotransmitter, or chemical messenger, that the brain produces when we do things we enjoy.

EMPATHY – the ability to understand and share the emotions and feelings of another being.

FAT – we use fat in our bodies as a source of energy, to keep us warm, to help us take in vitamins and to protect our organs. It's found naturally in animal products (meat and dairy) and in nuts, seeds, grains and fruits, such as avocados.

GRATITUDE – being thankful for the good things that happen to us.

IMMUNE SYSTEM – the body's defense against infections.

JUNK FOOD – food that contains lots of fat, salt, or sugar and few nutrients.

MEDITATION – a mental exercise that involves staying silent and calm.

MELATONIN – the "sleep hormone" that responds to darkness.

MINDFULNESS – paying attention to what is happening in the present moment.

MOLECULE – the smallest unit of a substance (like water), which can be divided into even tinier parts, called atoms.

NATURALIST – a person who studies or is an expert in plants or animals.

NUTRIENTS – the things we need from the food we eat (such as vitamins and minerals) to remain healthy and grow.

OXYTOCIN – a hormone produced by the brain that's associated with happiness and partnership. It's sometimes called the "kindness hormone" or the "love hormone."

POSITIVE-THINKING – a way of thinking that looks forward hopefully with a can-do, practical attitude.

PROTEIN – a substance that builds, maintains, and replaces body tissues.

SELF-ESTEEM – the way you think and feel about yourself.

STRESS – what you feel when you're worried or uncomfortable about something.

VITAMINS – nutrients that humans need to grow and be healthy. We get them from food and sunlight.

WELL-BEING – the feeling of being healthy, happy, and safe.

FURTHER INFORMATION

WEBSITES:

www.childline.org.uk – Great advice on feelings, making and keeping friends, and coping at school, at home, and with families.

www.healthforkids.co.uk – A fun website with great information about health, well-being and feelings.

www.rspb.org.uk/fun-and-learning/for-kids – Loads of ways to explore and enjoy nature, including tips on pond dipping and building a bug hotel.

https://thebekindpeopleproject.org – This website shows children and adults how to spread kindness by being kind to one another.

BOOKS:

You Are a Champion – How to Be the Best You Can Be by Marcus Rashford, 2021, Macmillan Children's Books

This Book Will (Help) Make You Happy by Suzy Reading, 2021, Wren and Rook

Grow Your Mind: Think Positive by Alice Harman, 2020, Franklin Watts

You Are Awesome by Matthew Syed, 2018, Wren and Rook

50 Ways to Feel Happy by Vanessa King, 2018, QED

INDEX